Pluto
IS PEEVED!

With thanks to Barbara Ann Porte —J.J.

To the outsiders, and anyone who has ever felt disconnected from the rest of the solar system —D.R.

Brimming with creative inspiration, how-to projects, and useful information to enrich your everyday life, Quarto Knows is a favorite destination for those pursuing their interests and passions. Visit our site and dig deeper with our books into your area of interest: Quarto Creates, Quarto Cooks, Quarto Homes, Quarto Lives, Quarto Drives, Quarto Explores, Quarto Gifts, or Quarto Kids.

2018 Quarto Publishing Group USA Inc.
Text © 2018 Jacqueline Jules

First published in 2018 by Seagrass Press, an imprint of The Quarto Group.
6 Orchard Road, Suite 100, Lake Forest, CA 92630, USA.
T (949) 380-7510 **F** (949) 380-7575 **www.QuartoKnows.com**

Seagrass Press titles are also available at discount for retail, wholesale, promotional, and bulk purchase. For details, contact the Special Sales Manager by email at specialsales@quarto.com or by mail at The Quarto Group, Attn: Special Sales Manager, 401 Second Avenue North, Suite 310, Minneapolis, MN 55401 USA.

ISBN: 978-1-63322-461-2

Digital edition published in 2018
eISBN: 978-1-63322-462-9

Printed in China
10 9 8 7 6 5 4 3 2 1

MIX
Paper from responsible sources
FSC® C104723
www.fsc.org

Photo credits: NASA/JHUAPL/SWRI (page 28); Uni Mannheim Mateo/Wikimedia Commons (page 29, top); Macrovector/Shutterstock.com (page 29, bottom); rijksmuseum.nl/collective/SK-A-957 (page 30); Hill Side Studios/gettyimages.com (page 31)

Pluto IS PEEVED!

AN EX-PLANET SEARCHES FOR ANSWERS

BY JACQUELINE JULES · ILLUSTRATED BY DAVE ROMAN

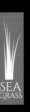

SEA GRASS

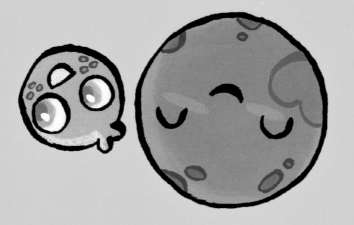

Of course I'm upset!

Oh, Pluto, don't tell me you're *still* upset!

I want to be *special*, like the big guys, Jupiter and Saturn.

That's because we live in the Kuiper Belt, Beyond Pluto. Beyond Neptune. We're a long way from the sun.

IT'S TOO FAR FROM THE ACTION.

PLUTO AND BEYOND...

Why not? What's wrong with here?

I don't like it here, Charon!

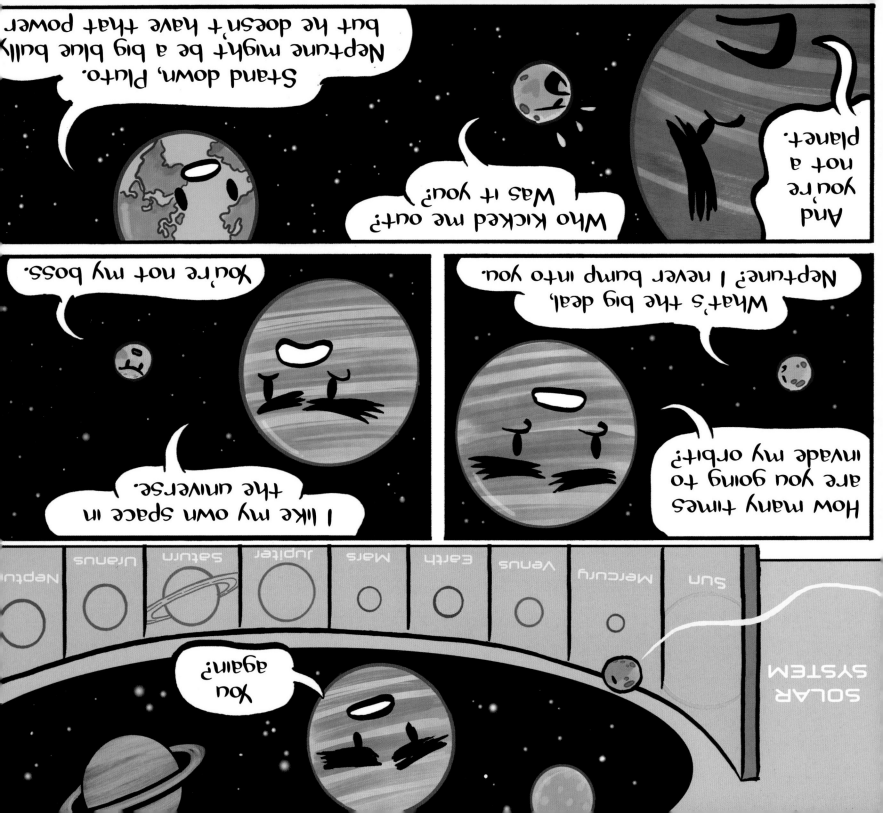

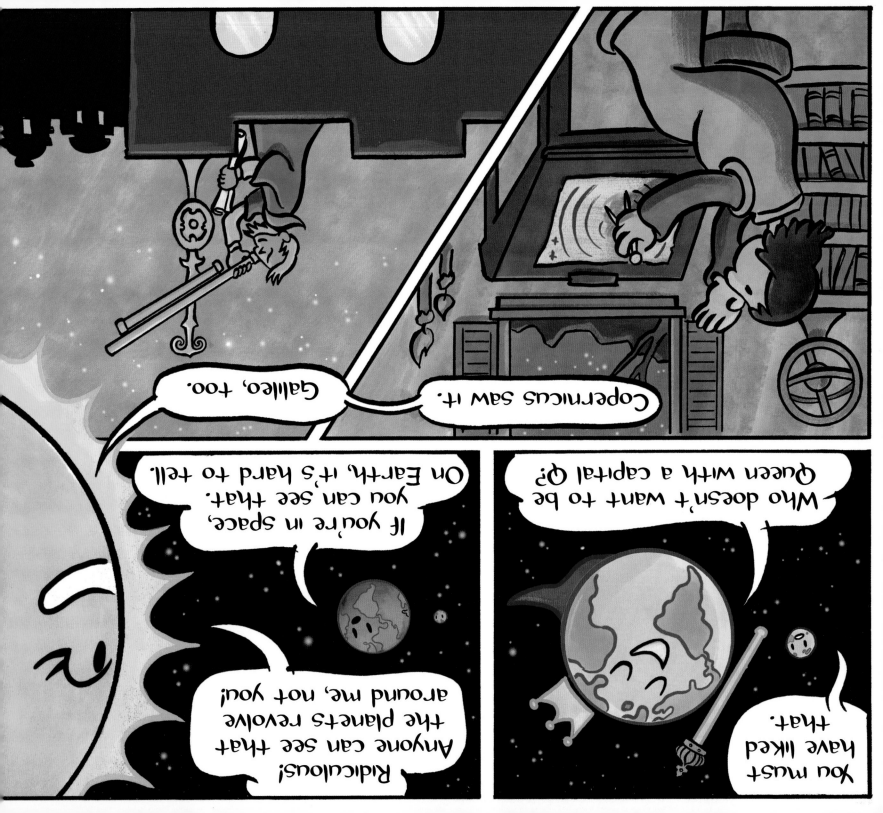

DINOSAUR HALL

What are you staring at?

A big bony creature with a very long neck!

That would be me.

hat's your name?

Hmmm. Interesting Question.

Why?

When I was discovered, I was called Brontosaurus. Then later on, scientists changed my name to Apatosaurus.

COME SEE
APATOSAURUS

At the Hall of Science!

COME SEE
BRONTOSAURUS!

BACK BY POPULAR DEMAND!

At the Hall of Science!

Now some scientists want to change my name back to Brontosaurus.

r it could have been a combination of things. Scientists are always busy collecting evidence to support theories.

'd like to know why.

You and me both. ut in the meantime, there is good news.

Scientists have found dinosaur fossils with feathers. Some of my relatives turned into birds. So I haven't completely disappeared.

Lucky r you.

Not just luck. Careful research. Scientists spend years studying my bones.

Why are you so interesting? You don't even exist anymore!

I was big. That gets attention.

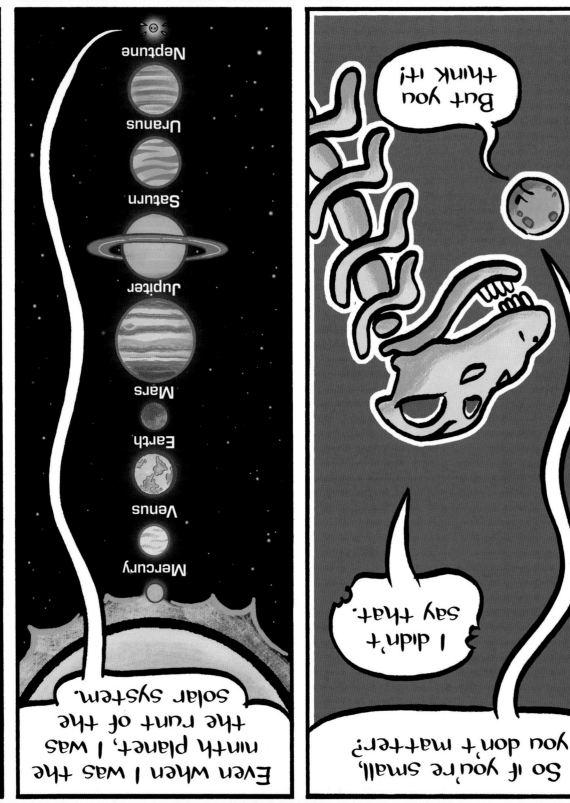

OUR MICROSCOPIC WORLD

SIGH...

What are these wiggly things?

They're so small!

We may be tiny, but we're important. Scientists study us day and night. Day and night.

That's puzzling. I just learned that science liked big things.

We're important! We're germs! Some of us make people sick.

ACHOO!!

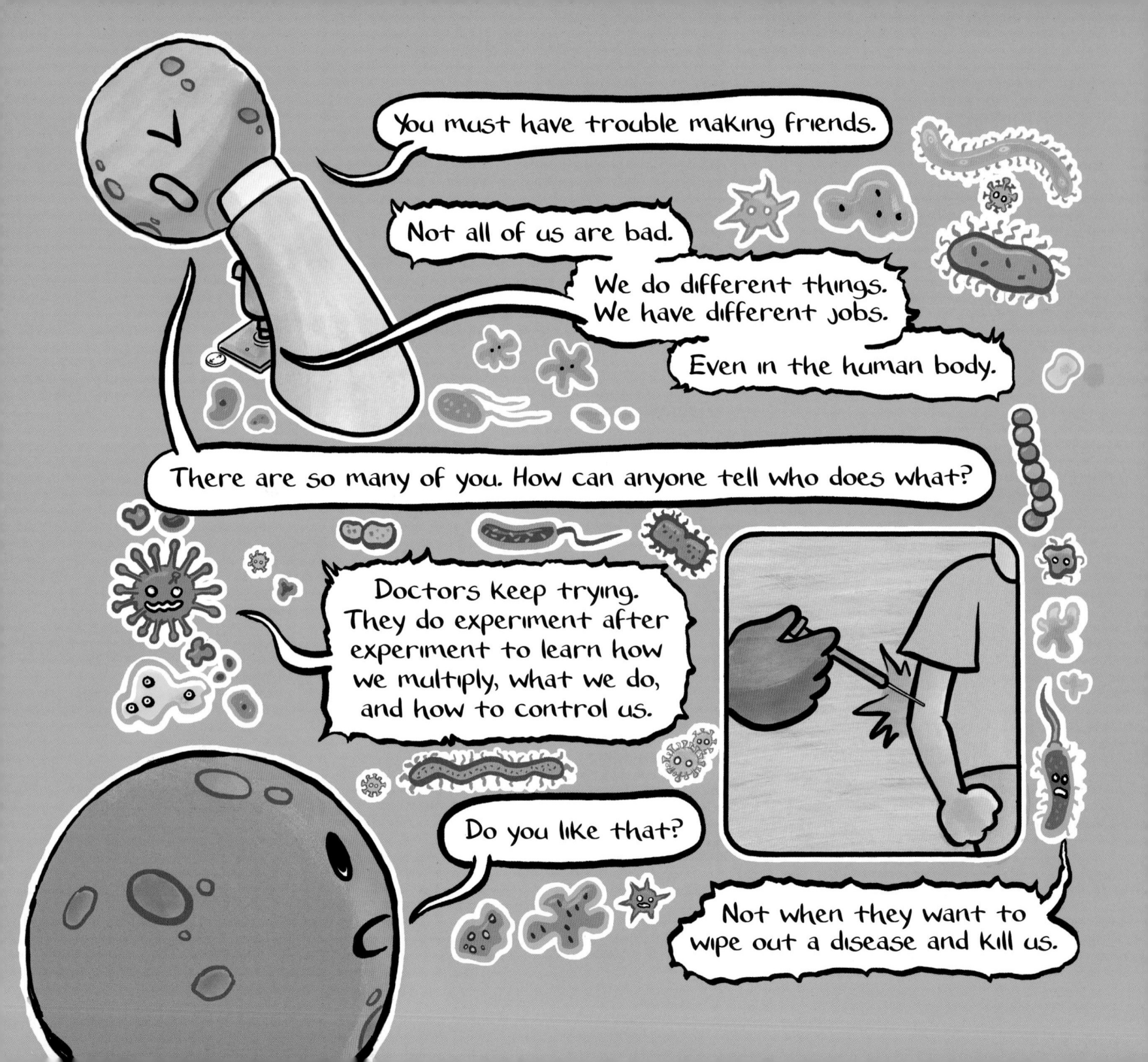

Pluto! We've finally found you!

I've got company tonight. You'll never guess who.

You're kidding me, right?

She's a spaceship called New Horizons. Her goal is to study the universe beyond Neptune.

Tell me about her.

You're Pluto? Wow! You need to meet my friend. She's in another exhibit. She'll be coming through for a visit any minute.

Pluto, the little guy in the Kuiper Belt who used to be a planet.

Who are you, anyway?

Is this a joke?

It's a dream come true.

What do you mean? Scientists don't care about me.

How can you think that? We're dying to learn more about you.

Since when?

Since always.

Scientists want to explore everything. Big and small. Dead and living. We're full of questions.

So am I! Why can't I be a planet?

It all began with an exciting discovery. An astronomer with a powerful telescope found something else in the Kuiper Belt.

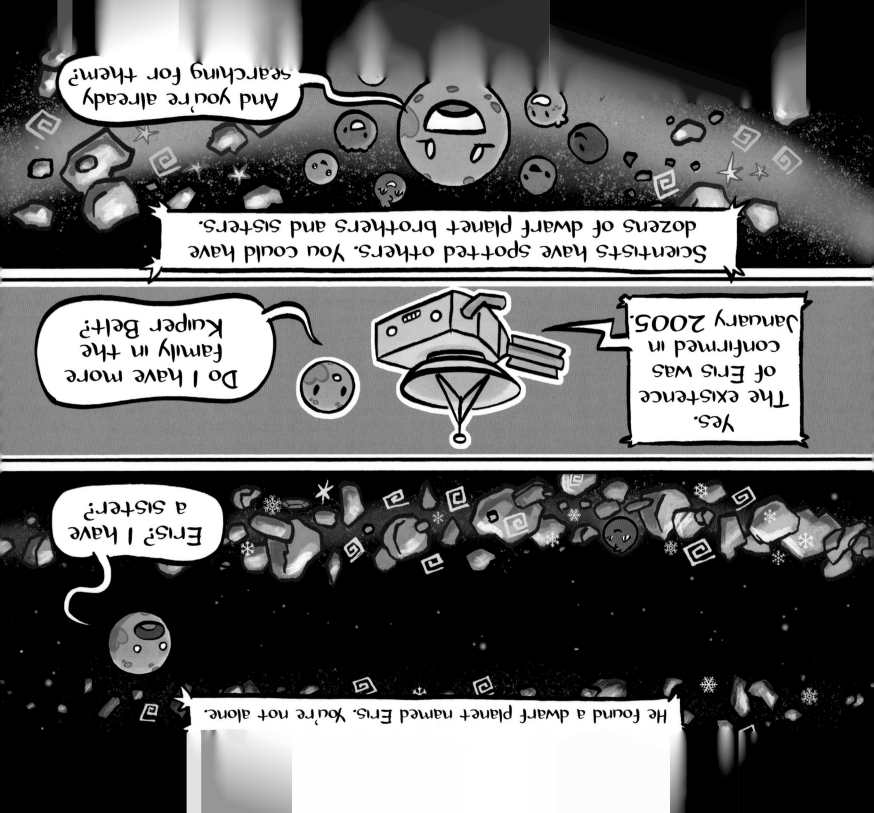

AUTHOR'S NOTE

For seventy-six years Pluto was considered one of a family of nine planets that orbited the sun. Teachers taught and elementary school children memorized a solar system with nine planets. In 2006 the International Astronomical Union changed the number of planets from nine to eight, leaving out Pluto. Pluto's change in status gives us a great example of how science works. When new evidence is discovered, scientists re-examine their conclusions. This has happened throughout scientific history. Before the Middle Ages and the work of Copernicus and Galileo, people believed that the sun revolved around the Earth. Until Louis Pasteur proved that germs were alive and could be killed, doctors did not have any idea how diseases spread. And of course, dinosaur fossils revolutionized our knowledge of prehistoric life.

Scientists make observations and question everything—even ideas people have long considered to be facts. It doesn't matter if something is big or little, dead or living. One question leads to another as scientists investigate, collect evidence, and expand our understanding of the world. With science, we develop the tools to make better lives for us all.

WHAT HAPPENED TO PLUTO

THE DEMOTION OF PLUTO: In 2005 Dr. Michael Brown, professor of planetary astronomy at the California Institute of Technology, announced the discovery of a round orbiting body in the Kuiper Belt. This sphere (later named Eris) was thought to be larger than Pluto, which had been discovered by Clyde Tombaugh in 1930 and is also a round orbiting body in the Kuiper Belt. The discovery of another round orbiting object raised questions. Did it qualify as a planet? Would every newly discovered orbiting sphere be considered a planet? This discussion led to a formal definition of the term "planet" by the International Astronomical Union (IAU) in August 2006. To be a planet, a celestial body now has to meet three qualifications: (1) It has to orbit the sun. (2) It has to have a nearly round shape. (3) It has to "clear its neighborhood," meaning that it has to be the biggest gravitational force in its orbital zone. While Pluto is round and orbits the sun, it does not have enough gravity to control its surrounding area; it does not "clear its neighborhood." The 2006 IAU definition of a planet put Pluto into a different category separate from

This composite of enhanced color images of Pluto (lower right) and Charon (upper left), was taken by NASA's New Horizons spacecraft as it passed through the Pluto system on July 14, 2015.

Earth, Jupiter, and the other planets in the solar system. This change did not, however, diminish the importance of the New Horizons space mission, launched by NASA in January 2006 to study Pluto and the Kuiper Belt.

THE CENTER OF OUR SOLAR SYSTEM: The ancient Greeks believed that the Earth stood still and that the sun, moon, and planets revolved around it. This Earth-centered view was considered to be scientific truth for centuries. In 1543 the Polish astronomer Nicolaus Copernicus published a book proposing the idea that the Earth and all the planets orbit the sun. Eighty-nine years after Copernicus died, the Italian scientist Galileo published a controversial book defending Copernicus's theory. Galileo suffered for this. He was put on trial for suggesting that the sun, not the Earth, was the center of our solar system. Today, the idea that the planets travel around the sun is considered common knowledge, thanks to a body of evidence compiled by Galileo and other scientists.

Nicolaus Copernicus

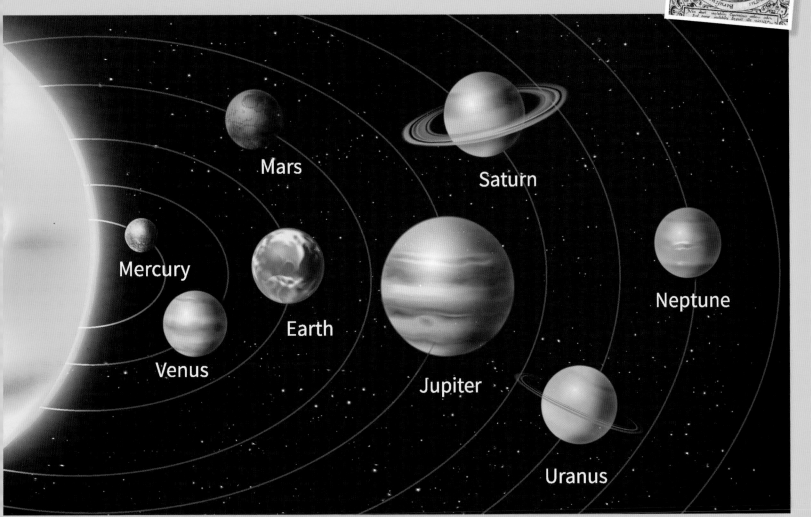

THE FATE OF THE DINOSAURS: Scientists are still studying why dinosaurs became extinct. A widely accepted theory says a huge asteroid struck the Earth, causing food to be scarce. Other scientists argue that climate and land changes could have played a role as well. Scientists learn about dinosaurs by digging for fossils and carefully studying them. They have changed their theories about dinosaurs many times. For example, the dinosaur brontosaurus, first named in the 1870s, was later reclassified as an apatosaurus. Recent research suggests, however, that the brontosaurus was actually distinct from the apatosaurus, and there is a call from scientists to resurrect its original name.

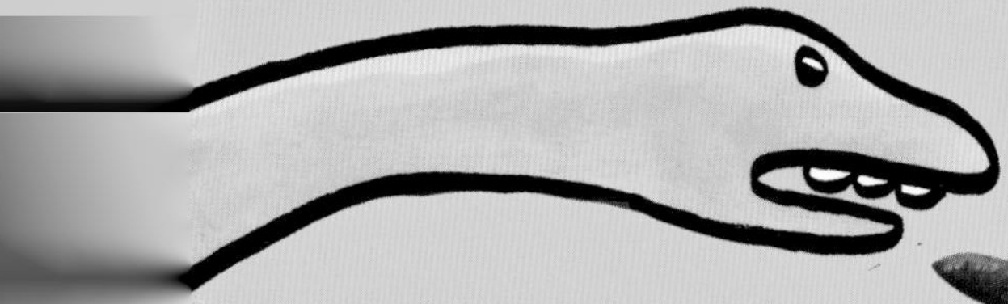

THE DISCOVERY OF GERMS: Tiny organisms were first seen under a microscope in the 1670s by a Dutch scientist named Anton van Leeuwenhoek. In a series of letters to the Royal Society of London, he described, with illustrations, tiny wiggling "animalcules." Some of these unknown microscopic creatures were bacteria. It took a long time for scientists to understand microbes. Louis Pasteur developed a system of heating, or pasteurizing, to kill germs in the 1860s. Medical scientists, sharing and building on one another's work, have discovered many ways of fighting the germs that make people sick.

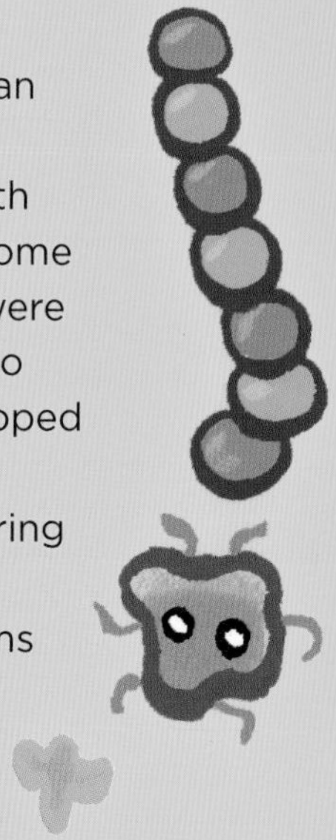

Anton van Leeuwenhoek

WHY STUDY ROCKS: Long ago, people believed earthquakes were created by angry monsters. Now we study plate tectonics to learn where earthquakes have occurred and where they may happen again. By researching rocks, we understand the composition of the Earth and how it was formed.

A NOTE ABOUT CHARON: Pluto's largest moon, Charon, was discovered in 1978. It is so large in relation to Pluto that some refer to Pluto and Charon as a double-planet. They orbit each other, which is also unusual. Could Charon's size and orbit prompt scientists to change its classification some day? We will have to wait and see.

GLOSSARY

ASTRONOMERS study the planets, the stars, and everything that exists in outer space. They use powerful telescopes to make observations, and they collect data from space missions and satellites.

EXPERIMENTS are conducted by scientists following careful steps under controlled conditions. Experiments can be repeated in the exact same way to see if they yield the same results. They provide measurable evidence and help scientists test theories and draw conclusions.

FOSSILS are the remains of animals, plants, and insects that lived long ago. They are found preserved in rocks, tar, and other places in nature. Scientists have collected and studied millions of fossils. They are an important source of information.

GEOLOGISTS study the materials that make up the Earth, such as rocks, oil, and minerals. They also research changes in the Earth caused by volcanoes, earthquakes, and floods.

PALEONTOLOGISTS dig up bones and other fossils to understand how prehistoric animals lived and what they ate. They want to know as much as they can about the animal and plant life that existed on the earth millions of years ago.

SCIENTIFIC THEORIES explain how something works in nature. Scientists develop theories after careful observation and experimentation.

SCIENTISTS ask questions, make observations, and collect data to gain a better understanding of how our world works. There are many different fields of science, and most scientists do their research in a particular area. For example, medical scientists study the human body and disease.

FOR FURTHER READING:

Alphin, Elaine Marie. *Germ Hunter: A Story about Louis Pasteur.* Illustrated by Elaine Verstraete. Minneapolis: Carolrhoda, 2003.

Aston, Dianna Hutts. *A Rock Is Lively.* Illustrated by Sylvia Long. San Francisco: Chronicle, 2012.

Bortz, Fred. *The Sun-Centered Universe and Nicolaus Copernicus.* New York: Rosen, 2014.

Brown, Mike. *How I Killed Pluto and Why It Had It Coming.* New York: Spiegel & Grau, 2010.

Kudlinski, Kathleen. *Boy, Were We Wrong About Dinosaurs!* Illustrated by S.D. Schindler. New York: Dutton, 2005.

—————. *Boy, Were We Wrong About the Solar System!* Illustrated by John Rocco. New York: Dutton, 2008.

Lindeen, Mary. *Investigating the Rock Cycle.* Minneapolis: Lerner, 2016.

Rusch, Elizabeth. *The Planet Hunter: The Story Behind What Happened to Pluto.* Illustrated by Guy Francis. New York: Cooper Square, 2007.

Steele, Philip. *Galileo: The Genius Who Faced the Inquisition.* Washington, DC: National Geographic, 2005.

Thimmesh, Catherine. *Scaly Spotted Feathered Frilled: How Do We Know What Dinosaurs Really Looked Like?* Boston: Houghton Mifflin Harcourt, 2013.

WEBSITES:

Gottesman Hall of Planet Earth: American Museum of Natural History, New York City
https://www.amnh.org/exhibitions/permanent-exhibitions/rose-center-for-earth-and-space/david-s.-and-ruth-l.-gottesman-hall-of-planet-earth

Hayden Planetarium: American Museum of Natural History, New York City
https://www.amnh.org/our-research/hayden-planetarium

Dr. Mike Brown's website: http://web.gps.caltech.edu/~mbrown/

New Horizons: NASA'S Mission to Pluto
http://pluto.jhuapl.edu/
https://www.nasa.gov/mission_pages/newhorizons/main/index.html
https://www.nasa.gov/feature/one-year-later-new-horizons-top-10-discoveries-at-pluto